PASSION

PASSION

A MUSICAL

Music and Lyrics by
Stephen Sondheim

Book and Direction by
James Lapine

THEATRE COMMUNICATIONS GROUP

Photographs by Joan Marcus.

ISBN 1-55936-087-9

Design and composition by The Typeworks.

Passion was originally produced on Broadway by The Shubert Organization, Capital Cities/ABC, Roger Berlind and Scott Rudin, November 9, 1994, by arrangement with Lincoln Center Theater. Sets by Adrianne Lobel, costumes by Jane Greenwood, lighting by Beverly Emmons, orchestrations by Jonathan Tunick, musical direction by Paul Gemignani and direction by James Lapine with Jane Comfort, associate director. The cast, in order of speaking, was as follows:

CLARA	*Marin Mazzie*
GIORGIO	*Jere Shea*
COLONEL RICCI	*Gregg Edelman*
DOCTOR TAMBOURRI	*Tom Aldredge*
LIEUTENANT TORASSO	*Francis Ruivivar*
SERGEANT LOMBARDI	*Marcus Olson*
LIEUTENANT BARRI	*William Parry*
MAJOR RIZZOLLI	*Cris Groenendaal*
PRIVATE AUGENTI	*George Dvorsky*
FOSCA	*Donna Murphy*
FOSCA'S MOTHER	*Linda Balgord*
FOSCA'S FATHER	*John Leslie Wolfe*
LUDOVIC	*Matthew Porretta*
MISTRESS	*Juliet Lambert*

Based on the film *Passione d'Amore,* directed by Ettore Scola, and on the novel *Fosca* by I.U. Tarchetti

PASSION

TIME
1863

PLACE
Milan and a remote Italian military outpost

SCENE ONE

Giorgio and Clara's room.

Drums. Lights slowly illuminate a bed with two figures who are making love on it. The woman (Clara) is astride the man (Giorgio).

Drums crescendo to a climax as Clara emits a soundless cry of orgasm, the orchestra substituting for her voice as the drums cease.

Music continues, murmuring underneath as Clara shudders a couple of times and falls into Giorgio's arms. A moment, as she lies back.

CLARA (*Quietly*):
> I'm so happy,
> I'm afraid I'll die
> Here in your arms.
>
> What would you do
> If I died
> Like this —

(She languishes across him)

Right now,
Here in your arms?

That we ever should have met
Is a miracle—

GIORGIO:
No, inevitable—

CLARA:
Then inevitable, yes,
But I confess
It was the look—

GIORGIO:
The look?

CLARA:
The sadness in your eyes
That day
When we glanced
At each other in the park.

GIORGIO (*Overlapping*):
We were both unhappy.

CLARA (*Overlapping*):
Unhappiness can be seductive.

GIORGIO:
You pitied me...

BOTH:
How quickly pity leads to love.

CLARA:

> All this happiness
> Merely from a glance
> In the park.
> So much happiness,
> So much love...

GIORGIO:

> I thought I knew what love was.

CLARA:

> I wish we might have met so much sooner.
> I could have given you—

GIORGIO (*Overlapping*):

> I thought I knew what love was.

CLARA:

> —My youth.

GIORGIO:

> I thought I knew how much I could feel.

CLARA:

> All the time we lost...

GIORGIO:

> I didn't know what love was.

CLARA (*Overlapping*):

> I've never known what love was.

GIORGIO:

> But now—

CLARA (*Overlapping*):
> And now—

BOTH:
> —I do.
> It's what I feel with you,
> The happiness I feel with you.

CLARA:
> So much happiness—

GIORGIO:
> You are so beautiful...

CLARA:
> —Happening by chance in a park.

GIORGIO:
> Not by chance,
> By necessity—

CLARA (*Overlapping*):
> Surely, this is happiness—

GIORGIO:
> —By the sadness that we saw in each other.

CLARA (*Overlapping*):
> —No one else
> Has ever felt before!

BOTH:
> Just another love story,
> That's what they would claim.
> Another simple love story—
> Aren't all of them the same?

CLARA:

No, but this is more,
We feel more!

BOTH:

This is so much more—!

(*Smiling at each other*)

Like every other love story.

Some say happiness
Comes and goes.
Then this happiness
Is a kind of happiness
No one really knows.

GIORGIO:

I thought I knew what love was.

CLARA (*Overlapping*):

I'd only heard what love was.

GIORGIO:

I thought it was no more than a name
For yearning.

CLARA:

I thought it was what kindness became.

GIORGIO:

I'm learning—

CLARA:

I thought where there was love
There was shame.

GIORGIO:
> —That with you—

CLARA:
> But with you—

BOTH:
> —There's just happiness.

CLARA:
> Endless happiness...

(*Music continues underneath as they lie silently next to each other for a long moment*)

> What?

GIORGIO: Not now...

CLARA: Tell me... please.

GIORGIO: I received my orders from headquarters. I've been transferred to the Fourth Brigade.

CLARA (*Sad*): When?

GIORGIO: I leave in five days.

(*Clara takes this news in, then slowly reaches for her chemise*)

GIORGIO: Though I'll be far away, we'll always have each other. Oh, Clara, please don't look so sad.

CLARA: You're the one who makes me happy.

(*She goes to the curtain and opens it; a brilliant shaft of afternoon sunlight fills the room*)

GIORGIO: We'll make the most of the next four days. We'll steal as much time as we can. And after I leave, we'll write each other daily. We'll make love with our words. You'll be with me every day, Clara.

(*She returns to Giorgio and begins to put on a stocking; Giorgio stops her*)

CLARA: I must go. I'm expected.

GIORGIO:
> God,
> You are so beautiful.
> I love to see you in the light,
> Clear and beautiful,

> (*Touching her lightly*)

> Memorize—

CLARA: No...

GIORGIO:
> —Every inch,
> Every part of you,
> To take with me.

CLARA (*Succumbing*): Giorgio...

GIORGIO (*Caressing her foot*):
> Your feet so soft,
> As if they'd never touched the ground—

CLARA: I can't...

GIORGIO:
> —Your skin so white,

So pure,
So delicate.

CLARA: Not now...

GIORGIO:
Your smell so sweet,
Your breath so warm.
I will summon you in my mind,
I'm painting you indelibly on my mind.

CLARA:
Let me go...

GIORGIO (*Moving up her body*):
We must fill every moment.

CLARA:
All this happiness
Ended by a word in the dark...

GIORGIO:
Oh my love, oh my darling...

CLARA (*Overlapping*):
So much happiness
Wasn't meant to last.

GIORGIO (*Caressing her*):
I am here,
I am with you,
I am yours.

CLARA (*Overlapping*):
I never knew what love was.

GIORGIO:
>Your skin,
>Your silken hair...

CLARA (*Overlapping*):
>I always thought I didn't deserve it.

GIORGIO (*Overlapping*):
>Your breasts,
>Your lips...

CLARA:
>I didn't know what love was.

GIORGIO (*Overlapping*):
>I want you every minute of my life...

CLARA:
>I don't know how I'll live when you're gone!

GIORGIO (*Enveloping her*):
>I will always be here.

CLARA:
>I don't know how I'll live...

(*Giorgio pulls her down next to him*)

>Giorgio...
>Don't leave me...

(*As they begin to make love again, military drums join the orchestra, quietly at first, then building in intensity to a climax. This time the drums drown the orchestra, and we segue into a military formation, which takes us into the Officers' mess hall*)

SCENE TWO

The dining quarters of the post's commanding officer, Colonel Ricci.

At center is a large dining table. At the back of the stage is a long staircase which leads to the living quarters.

Around the table sit: Colonel Ricci, a rather taut gentleman, who carries the weight of his position with authority and ease; Lieutenant Torasso, a man often given to laughter and opera singing; Major Rizzolli, a sober, straight-arrow type; Lieutenant Barri, a veterinarian with a love of gambling and not much else; and Doctor Tambourri, a somewhat aloof and distinguished older officer.

As the lights bump up, a Cook (Sergeant Lombardi) is overseeing the serving of the meal. Torasso breaks into an aria from "The Elixir of Love" while the others talk amongst themselves, ignoring him. After a beat:

COLONEL (*Having had enough*): Thank you, Lieutenant.

(*Torasso stops singing*)

DOCTOR: How was the opera?
TORASSO: Terrible. These touring companies get no better.

COOK: And neither do you.

TORASSO: I sing to lighten the impact of your heavy cooking.

(*They all laugh*)

BARRI (*Examining his plate*): Sergeant, what is this?

COOK: It's veal.

BARRI: Again? We had veal four days ago. And from the looks of it, it was *this* veal.

COOK: Lieutenant Barri, if I hear—

(*They are suddenly interrupted by a woman's distant scream upstairs. They pause momentarily before resuming their conversation, as if nothing unusual had occurred*)

RIZZOLLI: Colonel, I've heard a rumor that the King is about to sign a treaty with the French.

DOCTOR: Really?

COLONEL: I've heard no such rumor, Major.

DOCTOR: Where did you receive this information?

RIZZOLLI (*Uncomfortable*): In town.

COLONEL: You mustn't believe everything you hear in a whore-house, Major.

RIZZOLLI (*Serious*): That is where Garibaldi received much of his information, sir.

DOCTOR: Ah, so that's why you go there!

(*Giorgio enters*)

COLONEL: Ah, Captain Bachetti.

(*Everyone rises*)

Welcome. We wondered when you were going to arrive. May I introduce Doctor Tambourri, Major Rizzolli...

TORASSO: Lieutenant Torasso.
BARRI: Lieutenant Barri.
COOK: Sergeant Lombardi.
COLONEL: Please join us.

(*Giorgio sits; to his right remains an unoccupied chair and place setting*)

COOK: You'll have to excuse our limited menu, Captain. It's difficult to cultivate fresh vegetables in this mountain soil.
DOCTOR: We are not only isolated from life and ideas here, Captain, but anything green and edible as well.
RIZZOLLI: I just add vinegar to everything.
TORASSO: Captain Bachetti, the Colonel has told us of your triumphs pinning down the Russian infantry.
GIORGIO: I'm not sure my actions deserve your attention.
TORASSO: Didn't you rescue a wounded man in the midst of fire and then carry him on your horse to camp?
GIORGIO: Only to our battalion.
BARRI: Say you brought him back to camp! Why settle for being half a hero when full-fledged is just a white lie away?

(*The lights suddenly bump up; music under, agitated. Clara enters to the side of the stage, singing from a letter she holds*)

CLARA:
          Clara...

GIORGIO:
          Clara...
          I cried.

CLARA:
          I cried.

BOTH:

> Imagine that,
> A soldier who cries.

CLARA:

> I had to hide my eyes
> So the others on the train
> That carried me away from you
> Would think I was asleep.

(*We hear elegant Chopinesque piano music from upstairs as Clara exits; Giorgio looks up as lights restore*)

GIORGIO: Music?

DOCTOR: That's Signora Fosca playing.

COLONEL: My cousin. I have no family and neither does she. She is in such poor health, it's a continual worry.

DOCTOR: That's her place setting, but she stays in her room most days. Perhaps soon she'll be well enough to join us for a meal.

RIZZOLLI: She eats like a sparrow.

(*Torasso lets out an involuntary laugh, which is immediately stopped by a cold stare from the Colonel*)

TORASSO (*Sober*): My apologies, sir. The comparison struck me as funny. A sparrow seems to eat more than Signora Fosca. A pity it is...

COLONEL (*To Giorgio*): My cousin loves to read—it's her only passion, really. I can't find enough books for her.

GIORGIO: I also love to read. I've brought a few of my favorite books. I'd be most happy to lend them to Signora Fosca, though I can't promise they will appeal to her.

COLONEL: She's been given to reading military handbooks. I've no doubt she will welcome anything in print!

(Private Augenti enters and delivers a few letters, one of which goes to Giorgio)

AUGENTI: Mail!

RIZZOLLI: Nothing for me again? It's been two weeks.

AUGENTI: It smells to me as if Captain Bachetti has a letter from an admirer.

(Music under; the lights bump up. Clara reappears)

CLARA:
> Giorgio...
> I, too, have cried
> Inside.

BOTH:
> You must not be ashamed of your tears.

CLARA:
> I love you for your tears.

BOTH:
> Your absence only makes my love grow stronger.
> And when I cannot bear it any longer—

(Lights restore)

BARRI: Imagine surviving the battle of Alessandra only to lose your life to an aide-de-camp in a duel.

TORASSO: An aide-de-camp will do—

(We hear another scream come from upstairs. Music stops as Giorgio rises, concerned; the others continue to eat, unfazed)

COLONEL: Don't be alarmed, Captain. It's my cousin. I am so accustomed to her outbursts that I forget how unsettling they are to a newcomer. My apologies for not warning you.

DOCTOR (*Wiping his mouth*): A doctor is always expected to give some aid even when there is nothing one can possibly do.

TORASSO: Some more lamb, please.

DOCTOR (*To the Cook*): You've finally found some tarragon, haven't you?

COOK: Yes.

(*Another scream; the Colonel looks to the Doctor*)

COLONEL: Doctor.

DOCTOR: Excuse me.

(*He wearily rises and crosses to the stairs, which he climbs*)

BARRI: Sergeant, are there any more carrots?

COOK: Seconds for you, Lieutenant? Can I take that as a compliment?

BARRI: No, Sergeant, my horses are hungry.

(*Laughing, he gives Giorgio a slap on the back; Giorgio is not amused*)

COLONEL: In time, Captain Bachetti, you too will get used to life among us.

(*Snare drums; we segue outdoors. Clara enters while Giorgio oversees a formation of marching Soldiers; Clara sings from another letter, accompanied chiefly by drums and sporadic bugle calls*)

CLARA:

Clara, I'm in hell.

GIORGIO:

This is hell.

SOLDIERS:
> Living hell.

CLARA:
> Living hell.
> This godforsaken place—

SOLDIERS (*Overlapping*):
> This godforsaken place—

CLARA:
> This sterile little town,
> These pompous little men,

GIORGIO:
> This military madness...

SOLDIERS (*Overlapping*):
> This military madness...
> This military...

ALL (*Overlapping*):
> Uniforms, uniforms...

GIORGIO:
> Military madness...

SOLDIERS:
> Military madness...

CLARA & GIORGIO:
> My days are spent in maneuvers—

SOLDIERS:
> Uniforms, uniforms...

CLARA & GIORGIO:

My evenings in discussing the day—

SOLDIERS:

This is hell—

CLARA:

My nights are spent in thinking of you.

GIORGIO:

Don't forget me, Clara...

(*Clara exits as the Soldiers march off and the Doctor enters*)

DOCTOR: Good afternoon, Captain.

GIORGIO: Doctor.

DOCTOR: Your troops seem to be responding well under your command.

GIORGIO: Thank you.

DOCTOR: And how have you been enjoying our post, Captain?

GIORGIO (*Polite*): I find everyone most hospitable.

DOCTOR: Good. Your company at meals has been a welcome change for me.

GIORGIO: Thank you.

DOCTOR: I trust the occasional outbursts from Colonel Ricci's cousin have not unsettled you too greatly.

GIORGIO: What exactly is wrong with this woman?

DOCTOR: She is a kind of medical phenomenon, a collection of many ills.

GIORGIO: And those cries?

DOCTOR: Those are hysterical convulsions. One might say that her nerves are exposed, where ours are protected by a firm layer of skin.

GIORGIO: Is she in danger of succumbing to this illness?

DOCTOR (*Wry*): I don't believe so. Her body is so weak that it doesn't have the strength to produce a mortal disease.

GIORGIO: I don't understand.

DOCTOR: The weak protect themselves. The defensive soldier often lives longer than the brave one.

GIORGIO: Is she young?

DOCTOR: Late twenties, I would venture.

GIORGIO: Pretty?

(*The Doctor doesn't respond, but rather offers an enigmatic smile*)

You don't suppose that she is the lover of the Colonel, do you?

DOCTOR: Captain Bachetti, it's good to see that you enjoy an occasional bit of gossip.

(*Giorgio is immediately embarrassed*)

No need for discomfort, Captain. We're all human. Your curiosity is understandable. No, I'm afraid Signora Fosca's physical state prevents her from being anyone's lover. Good day.

(*He moves off; bugle calls*)

GIORGIO:
Clara, don't forget me.
Keep me close to you, Clara...

(*We segue back to the Colonel's dining room; it is morning. Rizzolli and Barri are finishing their breakfast as Giorgio joins them and sits*)

RIZZOLLI: Late for breakfast, Captain Bachetti.

GIORGIO: We had early morning exercises before the company departed for their weekly maneuvers.

(*The Cook enters and serves coffee to Giorgio*)

BARRI: You're a better officer than I am. I let my sergeant oversee the morning drill.

COOK (*Clearing Fosca's place setting*): Well, it looks as if Signora Fosca has disappointed us once again.

RIZZOLLI: Why keep setting her place?

(*Bugle call*)

BARRI (*Rises*): Captain Bachetti, I'm sorry we'll have to leave you to dine alone this morning.

GIORGIO: We still have dinner to share, gentlemen.

RIZZOLLI: Indeed we do.

BARRI: Any chance we might engage you in a game of cards tonight, Captain?

GIORGIO: I'm afraid I'm not a gambling man, sir.

RIZZOLLI: The boredom here will make a gambler of you yet.

BARRI: Good day, Captain.

GIORGIO: Gentlemen...

(*Rizzolli and Barri exit. Giorgio takes out a letter, which he begins to read. Clara enters*)

CLARA & GIORGIO:
   How could I forget you?

(*A shadowy figure [Fosca] appears at the top of the stairs and begins slowly descending*)

CLARA:

      Yesterday I walked through the park
      To the knoll where we met.
      Afterwards I sat on the bench
      Where we sat
      All that sultry afternoon.

      I thought about our room,
      Our little room,
      Where we were happy,
      And where we shall be happy again,
      Some day.

      I see us in our room,
      Our little room,
      And I don't feel so alone any more...

(*Against her song, the Chopinesque piano music which we heard before begins to play*)

      I close my eyes,
      Imagining that you are there,
      Imagining your fingers touching mine,
      Imagining our room,
      The bed,
      The secrecy,
      The world outside,
      Your mouth on mine—

(*Fosca descends the last step. She carries some books and approaches her empty place setting with an uncertain gait. As she turns from the shadows, revealing herself, we discover that she is an ugly, sickly woman: incredibly thin and sallow, her face all bones and nose, her hair pulled tightly back. Music holds*)

FOSCA:

    Captain...

(Giorgio sees her and is momentarily stunned. Clara exits. Fosca gives a nervous, grotesque smile as the orchestra resumes, playing the piano music. Giorgio quickly rises. Fosca speaks, in rhythm to the music; her voice is lovely and elegant, but melancholy)

I hope I didn't startle you.

GIORGIO: Signora Ricci, I'm Captain Bachetti—

FOSCA (*Simultaneously*): —Bachetti. (*A beat*) I know. My cousin has told me all about you.

(She hands Giorgio the books; he seats her)

I came to thank you for the books.
I would have sooner, but I've been so ill.

GIORGIO: Well, now you seem to be feeling more normal.

FOSCA (*Laughing tensely*): Normal? I hardly think so. Sickness is normal to me, as health is to you. Excuse me. I shouldn't speak of my troubles. I have been going through a period of deep melancholy.

(There is an awkward moment of silence as the Cook enters and pours her a cup of coffee. As he leaves, the music becomes low and intense)

I so enjoyed the novel by Rousseau.

GIORGIO: It's wonderful. My favorite, really.

FOSCA: The character of Julie is a great mystery.

GIORGIO: You should have kept the book longer to meditate over.

FOSCA:

I do not read to think.
I do not read to learn.
I do not read to search for truth,
I know the truth,
The truth is hardly what I need.
I read to dream.

I read to live
In other people's lives.
I read about the joys
The world
Dispenses to the fortunate,
And listen for the echoes.

(*Fiercely*)

I read to live,
To get away from life!

(*Calmer*)

No, Captain, I have no illusions.
I recognize the limits of my dreams.
I know how painful dreams can be
Unless you know
They're merely dreams.

(*Smiling aridly*)

There is a flower
Which offers nectar at the top,
Delicious nectar at the top,
And bitter poison underneath.
The butterfly that stays too long

And drinks too deep
Is doomed to die.

I read to fly,
To skim—
I do not read to swim.

(*Bitterly*)

I do not dwell on dreams.
I know how soon a dream becomes an expectation.
How can I have expectations?
Look at me.

(*As Giorgio starts to protest*)

No, Captain, look at me—
Look at me!

(*Exalted*)

I do not hope for what I cannot have!
I do not cling to things I cannot keep!

(*Tightly*)

The more you cling to things,
The more you love them,
The more the pain you suffer
When they're taken from you...

(*Calming down again*)

Ah, but if you have no expectations,

Captain,
You can never have a disappointment.

(*Gives a short laugh; music continues under*)

I must be mad to chatter on about myself like this to you.
Forgive me...

GIORGIO (*At a loss*): I assure you—

FOSCA: No, forgive me, please...

GIORGIO: But truly, there is nothing to forg—

FOSCA (*Overlapping; brightly*):
Have you explored the town?

(*Before he can reply*)

It is remote, isn't it?
And provincial, don't you think?

GIORGIO: Yes.

FOSCA:
And everything so brown:
The streets, the fields,
The river even,
Though there are some lovely gardens.

(*Anxiously*) You do like gardens, I hope?

GIORGIO: Yes.

FOSCA:
Good, I can show you gardens.

(*Giorgio smiles uncomfortably*)

And then of course there is the castle.

(*Giorgio looks blank*)

The ruined castle.

GIORGIO: Ah.

FOSCA: I find it lovely. Probably because it's ruined, I suppose.

GIORGIO (*Avoiding her intensity*): I didn't know there was a castle.

FOSCA:

> I like to take excursions there—
> When I'm in better health.

(*Giorgio smiles politely*)

> Perhaps you'll join me

(*As Giorgio tries to hide his discomfort*)

> And my cousin
> One day...

GIORGIO (*Trapped, as she stares*): That would be delightful. (*Lightly*) I don't believe I've seen a flower or a garden since the day I arrived.

(*Fosca suddenly gets up and slowly leaves the room. Confused, Giorgio rises and, after she has gone, takes his hat and books and begins to leave. We hear the distant sound of field drums, muffled, funereal. Fosca, just as unexpectedly, returns, carrying a small bunch of flowers, which she offers to Giorgio without a word*)

How very kind.

FOSCA (*Crossing to the window*): I'm surprised you haven't noticed our wonderful greenhouse.

GIORGIO: Greenhouse?

FOSCA: They've had no luck with vegetables, but the gardenias and petunias are magnificent.

(*Giorgio joins her at the window, as the drums become louder*)

GIORGIO: And to think how many times I've passed that building and not taken notice. (*Matter-of-fact*) Oh look. There's a hearse drawing up—it must be for flowers to adorn the casket.

(*Fosca stiffens and steps back, drawing her hand to her mouth, her eyes staring*)

It's good to know that the dead here—

(*Fosca begins to tremble*)

—can go to their graves...

(*Fosca lets out a terrible cry and collapses to the floor as Giorgio turns to her, stunned*)

Help! Doctor!!

(*Giorgio goes to her, but two female Attendants and the Doctor rush in and reach her first. Giorgio steps back, staring helplessly as they carry her off*)

How can I describe her?
The wretchedness,
God, the wretchedness
And the suffering,
The desperation
Of that poor unhappy creature—

The embarrassment, Clara,
Looking at that loneliness,
Listening to all that self-pity...

(*Another formation of Soldiers takes us to the Garden*)

SOLDIERS:
The town—
It is remote, isn't it?
And provincial,
Don't you think?
And everything so brown:
The streets, the fields,
The river even...

Of course there is the castle...
The ruined castle...

SCENE THREE

The castle garden.

The Colonel, the Doctor and Fosca enter and stroll through the garden down to Giorgio; music continues underneath.

DOCTOR: Look at how they've let this garden go.

COLONEL: This is not Milan, Doctor.

DOCTOR: I'm all too well aware of that.

FOSCA: I think it's rather beautiful.

DOCTOR: For these parts, maybe...

COLONEL: Doctor Tambourri, may I have a word with you?

DOCTOR: Certainly.

COLONEL: Captain Bachetti, would you lend my cousin your arm?

GIORGIO: Of course.

COLONEL: We'll catch up with you in a moment.

(Giorgio crosses to Fosca and lends his arm to her, trying to mask his discomfort. They stroll, as the two men head in the other direction)

FOSCA: I know how to walk. My cousin likes to treat me like a child.

GIORGIO:
>All the while as we strolled, Clara—

FOSCA: I hope I didn't frighten you the other day.
GIORGIO: No, not at all.
>—I could see you reading my letter.

FOSCA: I'm not afraid of death.

GIORGIO:
>All the while as we strolled—

FOSCA: I rather think I'd welcome dying. It's everything that follows that I dread: being shut up in a coffin, smothered in the earth, turning into dust. These images send me into a state of terror.

GIORGIO:
>—All I saw,
>—All I knew,
>All that I could think of was you.

(*Clara enters, reading a letter*)

FOSCA: Even talking of this makes me...

(*Momentarily, Giorgio fears she will suffer another attack*)

GIORGIO: Surely if you are sick, there is always the hope that you will get better.

CLARA:
>—All that I could think of was you.

FOSCA: Hope, in my case, is in short supply.

CLARA:
How ridiculous—

GIORGIO: Well then, one must look to life for whatever pleasures it can offer.
FOSCA: And what might they be?

CLARA:
—To be looking at her—

GIORGIO: Helping others, for example.
FOSCA: Helping others! (*Laughs*)

CLARA:
—And be thinking of you.

FOSCA: I have worked in poorhouses, Captain.

CLARA:
How could anyone—

FOSCA: I felt no different.

CLARA:
So unbeautiful—

FOSCA: Pity is nothing but passive love.

CLARA:
—Stir my memory of you?

FOSCA: Dead love.

(*Giorgio is silent as they walk, lost in reverie*)

CLARA:

> To feel a woman's touch,
> To touch a woman's hand,
> Reminded me how much
> I long to be with you,
> How long I've been without you near.
> And then to hear a woman's voice,
> To hold a woman's arm,
> To feel a woman's touch...

GIORGIO (*Noticing that Fosca is staring at him, snaps out of his reverie; music continues*): These thoughts are bad for you. You must concentrate on everything around you that suggests beauty and life. These trees, these flowers, the warm smell of the air—

FOSCA: You make it sound so simple, Captain. As if a flower or a tree could somehow make one happy.

CLARA:

> Perhaps it was the dress,
> The fragrance of her dress,
> The light perfume of silk
> That's warm from being in the sun,
> That mingles with a woman's own perfume,
> The fragrance of a woman...

GIORGIO: There is no absolute happiness in anyone's life, Signora. The only happiness we can be certain of is love.

FOSCA: What do you mean?

CLARA:

> The garden filled with you—

FOSCA: Are you speaking of friendships? Family?

GIORGIO: I'm speaking of a superior kind of love—

CLARA:
    —And all that I could do—

GIORGIO: —the kind between two people.

CLARA:
    —Because of you,
    Was talk of love—

FOSCA: Two people...
GIORGIO: Yes.

(Giorgio sings to Fosca as Clara continues to sing the letter)

CLARA & GIORGIO:
    —Love that fills
    Every waking moment,
    Love that grows
    Every single day,
    Love that thinks
    Everything is pure,
    Everything is beautiful,
    Everything is possible.

    Love that fuses two into one,
    Where we think the same thoughts,

GIORGIO:
    Want the same things,

BOTH:
    Live as one,

GIORGIO:
> Feel as one,

BOTH:
> Breathe as one.

CLARA:
> Love that shuts away the world,

GIORGIO (*Overlapping*):
> Love that shuts away the world,

CLARA:
> That envelops my soul,

GIORGIO (*Overlapping*):
> That envelops your soul,

CLARA:
> That ennobles my life,

GIORGIO (*Overlapping*):
> Your life,

BOTH:
> Love that floods
> Every living moment,
>
> Love like—

(*Giorgio hesitates, then turns back to Fosca*)

CLARA:
> —Ours.

FOSCA: Love like—?

GIORGIO (*As Fosca looks quizzically at him*):
  Like wine.

  An intoxication...

  (*Music continues under as Clara retreats and exits*)

  A great blindness, if you will.
FOSCA: Yes, I've read about that love, but you speak of it as one
  who lives it.

  (*Music stops. She stumbles slightly; Giorgio goes to aid her,
  but she pulls herself away*)

  I don't feel well. I must go back.

  (*Music resumes*)

GIORGIO: I'm sorry.
FOSCA: You can be incredibly cruel, Captain.
GIORGIO: Cruel?

FOSCA:
  To speak to me of love—

GIORGIO (*Nervous*): Forgive me. I didn't mean to speak—

FOSCA:
  To dangle words like "happiness,"
  "Beautiful,"
  "Superior"—
  You can't be that naive.

You with all your books,
Your taste,
Your sensitivity,
I thought you'd understand.

The others—well,
They're all alike.
Stupidity is their excuse,
As ugliness is mine,
But what is yours?

I've watched you from my window.
I saw you on the day that you arrived.
Perhaps it was the way you walked,
The way you spoke to your men.
I saw that you were different then.
I saw that you were kind and good.
I thought you understood.

(*Intensely*)

They hear drums,
You hear music,
As do I.
Don't you see?
We're the same,
We are different,
You and I are different.
They hear only drums.

All the time I watched from my room,
I would think of coming downstairs,
Thinking we'd meet,
Thinking you'd look at me,
Thinking you'd be repelled by what you saw.

(*We hear the Colonel and the Doctor in the distance*)

> Don't reject me.
> Don't deny me, Captain.
> Understand me, be my friend.
>
> They hear drums,
> We hear music.
> Be my friend...

(*Music under, fading*)

GIORGIO (*Stunned*): Yes. Of course. You have my friendship.

(*The Colonel and the Doctor approach; Fosca grabs Giorgio's hand*)

FOSCA: Thank you, Captain.
GIORGIO: Your hand is on fire.

(*Music stops*)

FOSCA: It's nothing. I have a fever.
COLONEL: Shall we make our way towards the castle?
GIORGIO: Signora Fosca is not feeling well.

(*The Colonel goes to her and takes her arm*)

COLONEL: I'm terribly sorry, my dear.
FOSCA (*Looking at Giorgio*): I'll be fine now.
COLONEL: Of course, but we should head back nonetheless.

(*Music resumes as the Colonel, the Doctor and Fosca head off with Giorgio trailing behind*)

SCENE FOUR

The dining quarters.
   Clara stands at one side of the stage with a letter in hand, Giorgio similarly opposite her.

CLARA: My darling, you did as you should. You had no choice.
GIORGIO: After all, her cousin is my superior.
CLARA: You must think of your career.
GIORGIO: How could I turn from such a desperate soul?
CLARA: You showed pity.
GIORGIO: Yet I have a sinking feeling.
CLARA: It is difficult for a man and a woman to be friends.
GIORGIO: I sense that she needs more.
CLARA: You must be careful to keep your intentions clear.
GIORGIO: I've opened the door.
CLARA: Desperation can take its toll.

   (Fosca is revealed on the stairs, descending; she also carries a letter)

FOSCA:
      Three days...

GIORGIO: Should I be cruel to keep myself free?
CLARA: There is nothing wrong with thinking of oneself.

FOSCA:
Three days...

GIORGIO: All I think of is you.
CLARA: Keep your distance.
GIORGIO: Yes, keep my distance.
CLARA: Make yourself scarce.
GIORGIO: Unavailable.
CLARA: Aloof.

FOSCA:
Three days...

GIORGIO: I love you so.
CLARA: I love you more.

FOSCA:
Three—

GIORGIO: Forever yours,

FOSCA:
—Days.

CLARA: As always,
GIORGIO: Giorgio.
CLARA: Clara.

(*Clara and Giorgio exit in opposite directions. Fosca reads from her letter as she crosses to the table. The dining hall, with its usual habitués, slowly comes into place behind her*)

FOSCA: Giorgio, these past three days have been perhaps the most painful of my life. I've looked for you everywhere. No matter how poor my health, I've made my way to the dining hall, praying you would be there. You promised me your friendship, Giorgio, but it's clear to me that your promise was a hollow one. I so looked forward to your company. Didn't you know how your absence would upset me? I wish that I could strike you from my mind and my heart. But I can't, Giorgio. You may disappear, but I will not.

(*She folds the letter and slips it under the napkin at Giorgio's place setting, then sits. Everyone follows and the scene comes to life*)

BARRI: ...I applied for a new pair of horses, but they only had bays or piebalds.
COOK: Piebalds!
TORASSO: You certainly don't want piebalds.
RIZZOLLI: Perhaps you should go to Turin. There's a wonderful stable there—
BARRI: No. That stable is no longer reputable.

(*Giorgio enters*)

TORASSO: Ah, Bachetti...
COLONEL: We haven't seen you in three days, Captain.
GIORGIO: I decided to accompany my troops on maneuvers.
BARRI: Your hard work is determined to give us all a bad name.
GIORGIO: Nonsense.

(*He sits and as he takes his napkin, the lights elsewhere darken. He discovers the letter and is about to open it when he looks to Fosca, who returns the look. He immediately*)

*sticks the letter into his pocket. The lights restore as he
begins to help himself to food)*

Excuse me, Doctor. Why do you always put that gold coin
on the table?

DOCTOR: For thirty years, I've done that whenever I eat with
other officers. The first meal where no one talks about horses
or women,

(As some of the other officers chime in)

I'll surrender my gold coin.

(Laughter)

BARRI: Some risk! You'll never lose it!

RIZZOLLI: I remember a wager that Lieutenant Barri made
once —

*(The lights suddenly change. Fosca grabs Giorgio's hand as
he reaches for the salt; she draws his hand by her side and
out of view under the table)*

FOSCA *(To Giorgio, whispering)*: I've missed you so.

GIORGIO: Please.

FOSCA: You must read my letter.

GIORGIO: Let go of my hand! Let go!

*(Giorgio tries to free his hand with no success; the lights
restore)*

RIZZOLLI: ...Well, of course there was no chance for anyone
but him to win.

BARRI: No one was forced to bet, Major.

DOCTOR: Please pass the salt.

(*Fosca passes it*)

Not hungry, Captain?

GIORGIO: Yes, yes.

(*He tries once more to free his hand without luck; agitated*)

Colonel, I've received a letter today.

(*Beat; Fosca freezes*)

I'm urgently needed in Milan. I request a leave of at least five days.

DOCTOR: What?

(*The table noise suddenly quiets*)

COLONEL (*Pause; annoyed*): If you had asked me this in my office, I might have refused. After all, you've been here only a month...

GIORGIO: I know, sir. It's of some importance.

COLONEL: I should hope. When do you wish to leave?

GIORGIO: First train tomorrow, sir.

COLONEL (*Beat*): Very well. At this table, who could say no to a guest?

TORASSO (*Laughing*): By this time tomorrow, you'll probably be in the arms of some young beauty.

(*The table fills once more with conversation as Fosca lets go of Giorgio's hand and dissolves into herself. Giorgio quickly turns from her and continues with his meal as the lights slowly fade to black.*)

In a ghostly fashion, the Soldiers perform their drill.)

AUGENTI, SOLDIER 1 & SOLDIER 2:
All the time I watched from my room...

AUGENTI:
Thinking we'd meet...

SOLDIER 1:
Thinking you'd look at me...

SOLDIER 2:
Thinking you'd—

AUGENTI, SOLDIER 1 & SOLDIER 2:
—Be repelled by what you saw.

SOLDIER 1 & SOLDIER 2:
Don't reject me...

AUGENTI, RIZZOLLI, BARRI & TORASSO:
Don't deny me...

AUGENTI, SOLDIER 1 & SOLDIER 2:
Understand me, be my friend.

ALL:
They hear drums.
We hear music.
Be my friend...

SCENE FIVE

The courtyard.

Morning fog covers the stage as military exercises take place. Giorgio enters with a suitcase in hand, salutes the Soldiers, then begins to cross the stage. The formation marches off as Fosca surprises him out of the shadows.

FOSCA: When will you be back?

GIORGIO (*Stunned*): What are you doing up and out at this hour?

FOSCA: When will you be back?

GIORGIO: You know I have a five-day leave.

FOSCA: Will you think of me when you're gone?

GIORGIO: Thinking of my work, my superiors, of your cousin, I will no doubt also think of you.

(*He begins to walk away but Fosca steps in his path*)

Please, Signora. Don't make this difficult.

(*He walks further, but she continues to block his path. He raises his hand to impede her; Fosca grabs it and presses it to her breast, then throws herself around him, planting kisses over his face and neck. Giorgio pushes her away*)

Please! You must stop this behavior immediately. What will people think if they see this display?

FOSCA: What does it matter if they see me? What do I care if the world knows how I feel? I adore you!

(*He tries once more to escape, but she drops to the ground and wraps herself around his legs*)

Is that something I should be ashamed of? Is that something I should hide? I'm no fool. I know you don't feel the same towards me. But one loves a dog, an animal. What can I do to get you to love me—a human being such as yourself?

(*She begins to weep*)

GIORGIO (*Trembling*): Get up, Signora, please. I beg you.

(*He helps her up*)

Compose yourself. Calm down. You see that I must leave right away. I am touched by your affection. It flatters me greatly. My mind races with a thousand thoughts.

FOSCA: Tell me your thoughts.

GIORGIO: Really, I must go.

FOSCA: Write me.

GIORGIO: Fine. I will write you. (*He starts to leave*)

FOSCA (*Holding him*): Promise.

GIORGIO: Yes, I promise.

FOSCA: Tomorrow.

GIORGIO: Tomorrow. Go. I want no one to see you here.

FOSCA (*Kissing his cloak*): Bless you.

(*She lets go and he races out. Music. Fosca crosses to her drawing room on one side of the stage while on the other side Giorgio and Clara's meeting place appears. Clara is in*)

bed. Silently, Giorgio comes to her and embraces her pas-
sionately as she begins to strip off his clothes. Augenti enters
Fosca's drawing room with a letter)

AUGENTI: Signora.

(*He exits; Fosca tears open the letter*)

FOSCA (*Reading*):
    I am writing to you,
    Signora,
    Just as soon as I've arrived,
    With a most unhappy heart.

GIORGIO:
    God, you are so beautiful—

FOSCA:
    I do not wish to cause you pain—

GIORGIO:
    As I remember every night—

FOSCA:
    So please consider what I say—

GIORGIO:
    Clear and beautiful—

FOSCA:
    With calm.

GIORGIO:
    —Every night, every day, every part of you...

FOSCA:
>My heart—

CLARA:
>You feel so good—

FOSCA (*Hesitating to read on*):
>My heart belongs—

CLARA:
>As if you'd never been away—

FOSCA:
>My heart belongs to someone else.

CLARA:
>Your breath so warm, your touch so sure—

GIORGIO (*Overlapping*):
>Your skin so delicate...

CLARA (*Overlapping*):
>Your arms so strong...

FOSCA:
>I am in love,
>Hopelessly in love—

>(*Increasingly upset*)

>Hopelessly in love,
>And am loved hopelessly in turn,
>Signora.

GIORGIO & CLARA:
>All this happiness—

FOSCA:
    You and I—

GIORGIO & CLARA:
    Being here with you in the dark.

FOSCA:
    —Were not meant for each other.

GIORGIO & CLARA:
    So much happiness—

FOSCA:
    If I seemed to imply
    Something more—

GIORGIO & CLARA:
    Even more than what I felt before!

FOSCA:
    —I apologize.

GIORGIO & CLARA:
    To feel your touch again—

FOSCA:
    But since we're forced to be together—

GIORGIO & CLARA:
    —When so much time has passed—

FOSCA:
    —Let us try to face the fact.

GIORGIO & CLARA:
    To dream of you and then

> To be with you again
> And have some time at last...

FOSCA:
> Let us both behave with tact.

GIORGIO & CLARA:
> How long were we apart—

FOSCA:
> If this letter seems cold-hearted—

GIORGIO & CLARA:
> —A month, a week, a day?

FOSCA:
> —It conceals my own distress.
> Nonetheless—

GIORGIO & CLARA:
> To feel your touch again—

FOSCA:
> —We must end what never started.

GIORGIO & CLARA:
> You've never been away.

FOSCA:
> You must recognize—

CLARA:
> Still, I've missed you—

(He puts his finger to her lips)

FOSCA:
> —There is nothing—

GIORGIO:
> Hush.

FOSCA:
> —Between us.

CLARA:
> —So much.

FOSCA (*Repeating*):
> Nothing...

GIORGIO:
> Shhh.
> I'm here now.

FOSCA:
> Nothing, nothing...

CLARA:
> Welcome home...

(Clara and Giorgio embrace passionately as Fosca, stone-faced, remains alone in her drawing room; her Attendants enter with a shawl, which they wrap about her, and a needlepoint frame, which she takes and begins feverishly working at.

Fosca's Attendants set the stage for Giorgio's entrance)

ATTENDANTS:
> I've watched you from my window.
> I saw you on the day that you arrived.

Perhaps it was the way you walked,
The way you spoke to your men.
You were different then,
You were kind and good.
I thought you understood...

SCENE SIX

Fosca's drawing room.
   Fosca sits doing needlepoint. She appears even sicker than usual. An attendant goes off and returns with Giorgio. Fosca greets Giorgio with a cold smile and signals the attendant to leave.

FOSCA: I received your letter and I thank you. I hope that we can still take hands.

   (*She extends her hand to him*)

GIORGIO: Of course. We can certainly be friendly.

   (*He takes her hand and bows politely over it*)

FOSCA: You don't know how mortified I am.
GIORGIO: Mortified?
FOSCA: About everything that's happened. My emotions some-times overpower my judgment.
GIORGIO: I found your affection very flattering.
FOSCA (*Smiling coldly*): How indulgent you are with me.

(She gestures for him to sit; he does)

Did you amuse yourself in Milan?

GIORGIO: Very much.

FOSCA: Admit that you only took leave to visit my rival.

GIORGIO: Your rival? *(Beat)* Yes, of course that was the purpose of my visit.

FOSCA: Excuse me. I can be so naive in respect to you. I should have understood what you meant by the "urgent need" that required your leave. And will you go back soon?

GIORGIO: Whenever I can. As soon as possible.

FOSCA: If you get another leave.

GIORGIO: Naturally.

FOSCA: Perhaps I should put in a word to my cousin. It all depends on him. Help from me might serve you well. Of course, a negative word...

GIORGIO: Place more value on your dignity. Don't offend your own pride, Signora.

FOSCA: We each deal with our pride as best we can. You love this woman very much?

GIORGIO: I wrote you...

FOSCA: Is she beautiful?

GIORGIO: An angel.

FOSCA: Then why don't you marry her?

GIORGIO *(Uncomfortable)*: She is already married.

FOSCA *(Taken aback)*: Aha! And you respect her?

GIORGIO: Respect has everything to do with love.

FOSCA: That's not true, but it hardly matters. And is your angel also a mother?

GIORGIO: Let's stop torturing each other. It's humiliating and unworthy of us. I find your sarcasm most distasteful.

FOSCA: I have many flaws, Captain.

GIORGIO: Our situation has been well-defined. Let's not discuss the subject again.

FOSCA: That's what I would like.

GIORGIO: Good. I hope we have no more occasion to speak of ourselves.

FOSCA: You can also hope that we will not see each other again.

GIORGIO: That may be the best course of action.

FOSCA: You may go now, Captain. I have more important things to do.

(*Giorgio rises, clicks his heels and exits. As Clara walks through, reading a letter, Soldiers and Attendants help us segue to the Doctor's office*)

CLARA:
>Three weeks...
>Three weeks...
My darling. The last three weeks have been a blessing. Signora Fosca has all but disappeared from my life here. She no longer has her meals with us or takes the occasional walk around the grounds. Even in her absence, I found myself hating her more and more. I've realized how I've had to temper my feelings towards her.

SOLDIERS & ATTENDANTS (*Simultaneously*):
>This is hell,
>Living hell,
>Living hell...
>This godforsaken place,
>This sterile little town,
>This military madness...

CLARA: But now that I'm free, I can feel as I please. But you, my Clara—you remain strong in my thoughts.

SOLDIERS & ATTENDANTS:
>Uniforms, uniforms...
>Our days are spent in maneuvers,

Our evenings in discussing the day.
Uniforms, uniforms...

(*Growing louder*)

Military madness...
Military madness...

(*Giorgio approaches the Doctor, who is at his desk*)

DOCTOR: Thank you for coming at this hour, Captain.

GIORGIO: Yes, of course.

DOCTOR: Signora Fosca has taken a turn for the worse. She is mortally ill.

GIORGIO (*A beat*): I am sorry to hear that.

DOCTOR: Don't you understand, my boy? It is because of you.

GIORGIO: Because of me?

DOCTOR: She told me everything. This was a confidence she made spontaneously, of course. You rejected her love—which doesn't surprise me—and now this refusal has increased the gravity of her disease. This woman is letting herself die because of you.

GIORGIO: Because of me! She is letting herself die! Then it is not a disease, is it, Doctor?

DOCTOR: She *has* an incurable disease, but if she is calm, if she takes care of herself, she could live for several years. This passion that has developed for you—

GIORGIO: Passion for me? Doctor, I hardly know this woman. She has thrown herself at me without cause.

DOCTOR: She does not think or act as we do, young man. As healthy people we cannot appreciate the psyche of the sick.

GIORGIO: Yes. Well, I am sure you will do all you can for her.

(*He begins to walk away but is immediately stopped by the Doctor*)

DOCTOR: A simple act on your part is all that is called for.

GIORGIO (*Turning*): I don't wish to get involved.

DOCTOR: You *are* involved, sir. Go see her.

GIORGIO: No.

DOCTOR: You, who saved a man in combat, must understand the need to save another's life when it is in jeopardy.

GIORGIO: How could I possibly visit Signora Fosca at her sick bed? It is improper. The Colonel would never allow it.

DOCTOR: You needn't worry. I have made all the arrangements.

GIORGIO: She knows of this business?

DOCTOR: You cannot imagine what this has cost her. You are a good-looking young man. Beauty is something one pays for, the same as goodness—another quality you embody. Please go to her now.

GIORGIO: And if I go, what next? What will she ask of me tomorrow or next week? You speak of what her feelings have cost her—but what have they cost me?

DOCTOR: I can imagine how difficult this is for you. But she is dying, and you have only to give her words. Words that will make her well. What is the cost of a few words when a life hangs in the balance?

(*A moment, then Giorgio exits as the Doctor watches*)

SCENE SEVEN

Fosca's bedroom.

A lone candle lights the stage; we see Fosca in bed. Giorgio tentatively enters the room and stands for a moment before a startled Fosca sees him and lets out a tiny cry; her hair is in a braid, her high fever giving her face a little color.

GIORGIO: No need to be frightened. It is Giorgio.

FOSCA (*Covering her face with her sheet*): Oh my God! My God! I never thought you would come. Of course I hoped...

(*She takes her arm from under the sheet and raises it in Giorgio's direction. He extends his hand which she grabs and kisses convulsively*)

I'm sorry. These are follies one commits before dying.

GIORGIO: Don't speak of dying, Signora.

FOSCA: Now that you're here, I won't. (*A beat*) Will you forgive me for having asked you to come?

GIORGIO: I am here because I chose to be.

FOSCA: Sit down.

(*Giorgio goes to a nearby chair*)

No. Sit here.

(*She indicates the bed; Giorgio stands frozen for a moment*)

Please.

(*He walks to the bed and gingerly perches next to her*)

Rest your feet on the bed.

GIORGIO: I am fine, Signora.

FOSCA: I want you to be comfortable. Please.

(*Reluctantly, he raises his legs onto the bed; she reaches for a candle, which she raises to his face*)

God, you are so beautiful.
Come, let me see you in the light.
No, don't look at me.
Let me look at you.
I feel better in the dark.

GIORGIO: Your kindness makes you beautiful.

FOSCA (*Surprised*): Do you value such beauty?

GIORGIO: Of course.

FOSCA: Do you think my heart is good?

GIORGIO: Yes, I do.

FOSCA: How do the good hearts beat? Can you distinguish them from the bad? Listen to mine.

(*Fosca takes Giorgio's hand and puts it on her heart*)

My heart says it loves you, Giorgio.

(*She places her hand on his chest*)

What does your heart say?

GIORGIO (*A beat*): It says it loves you, Fosca.

FOSCA: Like a...friend?

GIORGIO: Tonight it loves you as you wish.

(*He withdraws his hand and she does likewise*)

FOSCA: Thank you, Giorgio. I so wanted to forget you. To think that I could! I wanted to die without seeing you—

GIORGIO: I am here to tell you you'd be happier living.

FOSCA: That day I was so unpleasant to you—

GIORGIO: Please, let's not speak of the past. You are tired. Now that I have come, now that we have spoken, you must go to sleep.

FOSCA: Will you stay if I do?

GIORGIO: For a short while.

FOSCA: Will you sleep, too?

GIORGIO: If I can.

FOSCA: Put your head near mine. Can we dream together?

GIORGIO: Yes.

(*They close their eyes, as Clara enters*)

CLARA: My dearest Giorgio. It is three in the morning and I've just arisen from a dream of you, a dream so real I could swear you were there at my side. I am so used to this, having you in my dreams night after night. As I write this you are asleep. Do you dream of me? How I wish I could just lie by your side and watch you sleep. To see you disarmed, at peace. Sometimes I think that when you watch a person sleep there's a transparency that lets you see their soul. How I long to see yours...

(*Clara exits. Fosca wakes up and stares at Giorgio a*

moment before he wakes. She gently reaches out to touch his face)

FOSCA: It is you. I thought I was dreaming. Draw the curtain, please. I want to see the stars before the daylight takes them away.

(Giorgio gets up and complies)

Do you think there are worlds out there?
GIORGIO *(Staring into the sky)*: I do.
FOSCA: Will we ever visit them one day?
GIORGIO: I would like to think so. As a child I used to dream I could fly—travel to faraway places.

(He returns to her side; they seem more relaxed in each other's company)

FOSCA: Why is a man like you in the army, Giorgio?
GIORGIO: My father was an officer. It was expected that I would follow his path.
FOSCA *(She shakes her head, knowingly)*: Call me by my name.
GIORGIO: Fosca.
FOSCA: Say "Giorgio and Fosca."
GIORGIO: Giorgio and Fosca.
FOSCA: "Fosca and Giorgio."
GIORGIO: Fosca and Giorgio.
FOSCA: What music! *(Pause)* Do you love this woman very much?
GIORGIO: Don't ask me. I've told you how I feel.
FOSCA: What is her name?
GIORGIO: Clara.
FOSCA: Clara.
GIORGIO: Fosca, it will be light soon. I must be going.

FOSCA: Would you do me a great favor before you leave? Would
you write a letter for me?

GIORGIO: Certainly.

FOSCA: There is paper on my desk.

(*He goes to her desk and sits, taking up a pen*)

GIORGIO: Yes?

FOSCA (*Slowly*): My dearest...Fosca.

(*He stops writing and looks at her, annoyed*)

Please.

(*After a beat, he resumes writing*)

GIORGIO: "My dearest Fosca."

FOSCA:

> I wish I could forget you,
> Erase you from my mind.
> But ever since I met you,
> I find
> I cannot leave the thought of you behind.

(*Quickly, as Giorgio looks up*)

> That doesn't mean I love you...

GIORGIO (*Writing*):

> That doesn't mean I love you...

FOSCA:

> I wish that I could love you...

(*Giorgio stops writing*)

Please...

(*A brief pause; Giorgio resumes writing*)

I know that I've upset you.
I know I've been unkind.
I wanted you to vanish from sight,
But now I see you in a different light,
And though I cannot love you,
I wish that I could love you.

For now I'm seeing love
Like none I've ever known,
A love as pure as breath,
As permanent as death,
Implacable as stone.
A love that, like a knife,
Has cut into a life
I wanted left alone.

A love I may regret,
But one I can't forget.

I don't know how I let you
So far inside my mind,
But there you are and there you will stay.
How could I ever wish you away?
I see now I was blind.

And should you die tomorrow,
Another thing I see:
Your love will live in me.

(*As the music fades*)

I remain always...Your Giorgio...

(*He signs the letter and blots it*)

Please bring it to me.

(*He does*)

Thank you, Giorgio. Do you have sisters?
GIORGIO: Yes.
FOSCA: Do you kiss them goodbye?
GIORGIO: On occasion.
FOSCA: Kiss me goodbye the way you do them.

(*Giorgio gives her a peck on the forehead*)

No, like you kiss her.

(*Fosca suddenly pulls Giorgio to her and embraces him like a lover. Stunned, he pulls himself away; agitated*)

Now go! Thank you, Giorgio. Quickly! Run!

(*Giorgio runs from the room. There is a moment of calm and then Fosca lets out an involuntary scream; blackout*)

SOLDIERS:
    How can I describe her?
    The wretchedness,
    God, the wretchedness
    And the suffering, the desperation
    Of that poor, unhappy creature—
    The embarrassment...

Scene Three: Fosca (Donna Murphy) at the castle garden.

Scene Five: Giorgio (Jere Shea) meets Clara (Marin Mazzie) in Milan.

Scene Six: Fosca (Donna Murphy) awaits Giorgio in her parlor.

Scene Eight: The Soldiers (William Parry, George Dvorsky, Francis Ruivivar, Cris Groenendaal, Marcus Olson) gossip as they play billiards.

Scene Nine: Clara (Marin Mazzie) sings a letter to Giorgio.

Scene Eleven: Giorgio (Jere Shea), a blanket around him as he rides the train to Milan.

Scene Thirteen: A Christmas Party in the Colonel's quarters (Marcus Olson, Cris Groenendaal, Francis Ruivivar, George Dvorsky).

Scene Fourteen: Fosca (Donna Murphy) and Giorgio (Jere Shea) in her bedroom.

Scene Sixteen: Finale (Marcus Olson, Matthew Porretta, Marin Mazzie, John Leslie Wolfe).

70

SCENE EIGHT

Billiard room.

   Lights up as the men gather, play pool, Rizzolli and Torasso against Barri and Augenti; the Cook stands and watches; the Doctor observes them from the side.

TORASSO:
   Did you hear that scream last night?

AUGENTI:
   Did anybody not?

RIZZOLLI: Four-ball in the side.

COOK:
   She knows how to scream, all right.

BARRI (*As Rizzolli shoots*):
   Well, she practices a lot.

AUGENTI: Good shot.
RIZZOLLI: Six-ball in the corner.

COOK:
> So that wasn't dying, we assume.

BARRI:
> No, I think she just fell off her broom.

TORASSO:
> Or they hung a mirror in the room
> Of la Signora!

BARRI:
> La Signora!

AUGENTI:
> La Signora!

RIZZOLLI: Please, a little quiet!

(Bugle call. Drums continue softly under as the game continues; Giorgio enters to speak with the Doctor)

GIORGIO: Doctor.
DOCTOR: Captain.
GIORGIO: Was it truly necessary for me to go to her last night?
DOCTOR: Why else would I have asked you to go? I'm not some kind of procurer, Captain.
GIORGIO: She hardly seemed near death.
DOCTOR: I'm sure she summoned her strength for you. Her condition was precarious before you arrived. You have done her a great service. You have done a brave thing. Now it is over. Good day.

(The Doctor exits)

RIZZOLLI: Care to play, Captain?
GIORGIO: No. Thank you for asking.

(*He leaves; music resumes over drums*)

TORASSO:
> Just a bit aloof, don't you think?

COOK:
> Not around the Colonel.

RIZZOLLI:
> Gentlemen, gentlemen...

AUGENTI:
> Never trust a man who doesn't drink.

TORASSO:
> And he keeps a journal.

BARRI: Eight-ball off the nine.

RIZZOLLI:
> Maybe, though, he just prefers his books.

COOK:
> Not as much as he prefers his looks.

TORASSO:
> Which is why he thinks he's got his hooks
> Into la Signora—

(*Barri makes a spectacular shot, ending the game; sighs of admiration and disappointment from the others*)

BARRI:
> Gentlemen, I'll make a wager:
> Come the summer, he'll be Major—

(Bugle. Pause, as they look at each other and decide not to take the bet)

RIZZOLLI:
   I'll say!

ALL *(Except Rizzolli)*: I'll say!

ALL:
   I'll say!

(Music stops.
   As the billiard table disappears, we segue to the other side of the stage where the Colonel and Giorgio stroll in)

COLONEL: Captain, I cannot thank you enough. Your kindnesses to my cousin have meant a great deal.
GIORGIO *(Uncomfortable)*: You have no reason to thank me.
COLONEL: Any attention that is paid to her means so much. Signora Fosca has always had a shortage of friends.

(Fosca is revealed at her writing table)

FOSCA: My dear Giorgio. I am writing you even though the Doctor has forbidden it. What a joy to have someone to whom I can tell my feelings, with whom I can share my past.
COLONEL: I was a young man when my parents died and Fosca's mother and father welcomed me into their house whenever I was on leave.

(Music under, as we go back in time)

   As a child—

FOSCA:
>As a child—

COLONEL:
>She was lonely—

FOSCA:
>I was happy—

COLONEL:
>Her parents doted on her—

FOSCA (*Overlapping*):
>My parents doted on me—

>(*Fosca's Mother and Father enter*)

FOSCA & COLONEL:
>They said:

MOTHER & FATHER:
>Beautiful.

MOTHER:
>So sensitive.

MOTHER & FATHER:
>So beautiful.

FOSCA:
>They told me to be:

MOTHER:
>Careful—

COLONEL:
Of course—

MOTHER:
—Fosca.

COLONEL:
—To them she was.

FATHER:
A girl as beautiful as you are
Has to—

FOSCA:
And so—

FATHER:
—Be careful.

FOSCA:
I thought that I was beautiful.

FOSCA & COLONEL:
And then I (she) reached the age
Where being beautiful
Becomes the most important thing
A woman can be.

(*Fosca rises and crosses downstage*)

COLONEL:
An unattractive man—

FOSCA:
As long as you're a man,
You still have opportunities.

COLONEL (*Simultaneously*):
—Can still have opportunities.

MOTHER & FATHER:
Beautiful...

FOSCA & COLONEL:
Whereas, if you're a woman,
You either are a daughter or a wife.

MOTHER & FATHER:
A woman is a flower.

FOSCA & COLONEL:
You marry—

FATHER:
—Now you're seventeen.

COLONEL:
—Or you're a daughter all your life.

MOTHER & FATHER:
Now is the hour...

COLONEL:
I'd met this nice young man.

FOSCA:
I'd seen this nice young man—

COLONEL:
He'd introduced himself—

FOSCA:
—Passing by—

COLONEL:
—At my club.

FOSCA:
—Just below my window.

COLONEL:
So—

FOSCA:
One day—

COLONEL:
—One evening I invited him—

FOSCA:
—He tipped his hat to me.

COLONEL:
—Home.

(*Brings Ludovic, the young man of whom he has just spoken, over to Fosca's Mother and Father, as music continues under; Giorgio stands to one side and observes*)

Count Ludovic—

FOSCA:
I must admit that I was flattered—

COLONEL: —this is my Aunt Theresa and my Uncle Bruno.

(*The orchestra stops momentarily*)

MOTHER: A count?

FATHER: From where, if I may ask.

LUDOVIC: Austria.

MOTHER & FATHER (*Thrilled*):
 Austria...

MOTHER: What a beautiful place.

COLONEL (*Calling*): Fosca, we have a visitor!

FOSCA:
 Imagine my surprise...

COLONEL: I'd like you to meet a new friend. Count Ludovic.

(*Ludovic takes Fosca's hand and kisses it*)

FOSCA: He was even more handsome up close.

COLONEL: I was amazed to see the Count take such an interest
 in my cousin.

(*Ludovic crosses to Fosca and takes her hand*)

LUDOVIC (*Floridly*):
 If I had known you were here, Signorina—

FOSCA: "If he had known..." Of course he knew.

LUDOVIC:
 —I would have brought you many flowers.

COLONEL: If I had known...

LUDOVIC:
 You do like flowers?

FOSCA: Yes.

COLONEL:
>I should have known.

LUDOVIC:
>I've seen you at your window.

MOTHER: Won't you stay for dinner—?
FATHER: Do. Yes.

LUDOVIC (*Still to Fosca*):
>I've watched you every day since I arrived.

FOSCA:
>I had my suspicions.

COLONEL:
>I had no suspicion.

FOSCA & COLONEL:
>I chose not to see.

LUDOVIC:
>The way you move,
>The way you gaze at the sky...

FOSCA:
>For love had made me blind—

COLONEL:
>How could I be so blind?

FOSCA:
>—Or what I took for love.

COLONEL: Within a month, he had asked for her hand.

GIORGIO: Signora Fosca has been married?

COLONEL: Yes.

MOTHER & FATHER (*To each other*):
> Austria...
> Count Ludovic of Austria...

FOSCA:
> I sensed in him a danger,
> Deception,
> Even violence.
> I must admit to some degree
> That it excited me.

MOTHER & FATHER:
> Austria...
> Count Ludovic of Austria...

(*Music continues under*)

COLONEL: Once they were married, once he'd received my uncle's sizable dowry, he traveled a great deal, was unavailable to Fosca.

FOSCA: He gambled away the dowry.

COLONEL: It didn't take him long to spend all their money.

FOSCA: I was forced to go to my parents to borrow from what little savings they had left.

COLONEL: Then one day, as she was coming from market...

(*Ludovic's Mistress suddenly appears*)

MISTRESS: Excuse me? You're the wife of a Count Ludovic?

FOSCA: Yes.

MISTRESS:
You fool.
The man's a fraud,
A fake.
The trips he said he had to take
Abroad,
He took them so that he
Could be
With me.

He calls himself a Count,
But he's not.
He's never had a title in his life!
He doesn't have a title,
But he does have a wife
And a child
In Dalmatia.

FOSCA: No, you must be mistaken.
MISTRESS: Oh, yes.
He only wants to bleed you.
Until the day he doesn't need you.
I warn you he'll abandon you
As he abandoned her
And me,
And countless others, I've no doubt.
I'm telling you, the man was born without
A heart.

(*Starts away; turns back*)

You fool...

(*Exits, as Ludovic enters elsewhere; music continues under*)

FOSCA: I confronted him with this information, and he made
no attempt to deny it.

LUDOVIC (*Shrugging, pleasantly*):
Ah well, at last you know the truth,
Signorina.
But you as well must face the truth.
I've no desire to deceive you any more,
But do admit what you ignore:
We made a bargain, did we not?
And we got
What we bargained for.

(*The music becomes a waltz*)

You gave me your money, I gave you my looks
And my charm.
And my arm.
I would say that more than balances the books.
Where's the harm?
Now it's through.

If women sell their looks,
Why can't a man,
If he can?
Besides, the money wasn't even yours,
It belonged to those ridiculous old bores,
Your parents.

(*Fosca starts to strike him, but he catches her arm; smiling*)

Forgive me, my dear,
But though you are no beauty, I fear
You are not quite the victim you appear.

Well, let us part by mutual consent
And be content.
And so good luck and goodbye.
I must go.

(*Starts off; turns back*)

Oh, and yes, we haven't paid the rent
Since July...
Just so you know...

(*Exits, as music continues underneath*)

FOSCA: I returned home, to find my parents impoverished and
in poor health.
COLONEL: Fosca's health failed...
FOSCA (*Bitter*):
A woman's like a flower...

(*She returns to her writing desk*)

COLONEL: ...She began to suffer her first convulsions. My aunt
and uncle nursed her as best they could.

FOSCA:
A flower's only purpose is to please...

COLONEL: I spent months looking for the man.

FOSCA:
Beauty is power...

COLONEL: By then, of course, he'd vanished.

FOSCA:
> Longing a disease...

COLONEL: To this day, I dream of finding him and realizing my revenge.

FOSCA: My father died not long thereafter.

COLONEL:
> How could I be so blind.

FOSCA:
> I couldn't face the world.

COLONEL:
> It took her many months to leave her bed.

FOSCA (*Simultaneously*):
> It took me months to leave my bed.

COLONEL: When her mother died, she had nothing really. No one.

FOSCA: And so I went to stay with my cousin, who in some way felt responsible for my circumstances.

COLONEL:
> Why could I not admit the truth?
> How could I not have seen through the veneer?
> I told myself, "As long as she seems happy,
> Why interfere?"
> Or was I just relieved to know
> That somebody would want her for a wife?
> In war you know the enemy,
> Not always so in life.

The enemy was love—
Selfishness really, but love.
All of us blinded by love
That makes everything seem possible.

You have to pay a consequence
For things that you've denied.
This is the thorn in my side.

(*Music continues under, as Mistress, Mother, Father and Ludovic appear in tableau*)

MISTRESS:
As long as you're a man,
You're what the world will make of you.

MISTRESS & MOTHER:
Whereas if you're a woman,
You're only what it sees.

COLONEL, FATHER & LUDOVIC:
A woman is a flower
Whose purpose is to please.

ALL (*Except Giorgio and Fosca*):
Beauty is power,
Longing a disease...

(*As we segue to the next scene, Clara enters in a robe, her hair down*)

SCENE NINE

The mountainside, a distance from the outpost.

CLARA:
> Giorgio,
> I stand here
> Staring at the sunrise,
> Thinking that we've never seen a sunrise together,
> Thinking that the sunrise
> Only means another day
> Without you,
> And thinking:
>
> Can our love survive
> So much separation,
> Keep itself alive,
> Much less thrive?

(Giorgio walks onstage and sits; he takes a letter from his uniform pocket and reads. We hear the faint rumblings of thunder)

If only you were here,
If I could feel your touch,
I wouldn't have such fear.
If only we had more than letters
Holding us together,
If we just could hold each other now,
The sunrise then could be
A thing that I could see
And merely think, "How beautiful..."

CLARA & GIORGIO (*As Clara exits*):
Giorgio,
I now sit
Staring at the mirror—
You may not believe it but I swear,
As I stare,
There it is,
Plain as day:
A gray
Hair,

GIORGIO:
Of which I was unaware,
Which is more than I can bear,
Which I'm ripping out right now
And am sending on to you
As a milestone of my age,
As a turning of the page...

Perhaps when next we meet,
I'll be a sorry sight.
You won't know who I am.
My hair completely white,
My face
A mass of wrinkles.

What will you feel then,
My Giorgio?
Time is now our enemy...

(*Unsteadily, Fosca has entered and made her way towards Giorgio*)

FOSCA: You came a great distance to read her letters. Are you running away from me?

(*Giorgio doesn't respond; he returns the letter to his pocket*)

Since I've recovered, you've made every effort to get away from me. To be free of my company.

GIORGIO: There are times when I wish to be alone.

FOSCA: I know that I offend you.

GIORGIO: No. I won't have this conversation.

FOSCA: And what kind of conversation do you desire, Captain? Something innocuous? Do you wish to discuss your troops? Or should we talk about the weather? Feels like rain, what do you think?

GIORGIO: I think you can be very difficult.

FOSCA: I didn't come here to be difficult. I came here simply to share your company.

(*He notices blood on her hands*)

GIORGIO: What's happened to your hands?

FOSCA (*Looking at them blankly*): I must have fallen.

GIORGIO (*Attending to her hands*): You have no business being out here.

FOSCA (*After a beat*): Do you want me dead?

GIORGIO (*Walking away from her*): Fosca, don't be so unfair.

FOSCA (*Following him*): You're right, I am unfair. I want to free you from my affection. I know what I'm doing to you.

(There is a long, painful moment of silence as they sit and stare off into space)

Why is it that the violets and daisies blossom now?

GIORGIO *(A beat)*: They mistake Autumn's warmth for April.

FOSCA: What is that bird that sings?

GIORGIO: A wren, I think.

FOSCA: What does it look like?

GIORGIO: It's grey and I believe it's the smallest of birds.

FOSCA: The smallest...You know so much. *(A beat)* Give me a kiss.

(Giorgio recoils)

Yes, I know a woman shouldn't ask such a thing. A woman shouldn't have followed a man here. Well, given my appearance, I don't behave as other women do. And so I ask you for a kiss.

(He doesn't respond)

Then I'll kiss you.

(She takes his hand and kisses it)

GIORGIO *(Agitated)*:
    Is this what you call love?
    This endless and insatiable
    Smothering
    Pursuit of me,
    You think that this is love?

(Softly, attempting to control himself)

I'm sorry that you're lonely,
I'm sorry that you want me as you do.
I'm sorry that I fail to feel
The way you wish me to feel,

(*Growing in anger*)

I'm sorry that you're ill,
I'm sorry you're in pain,
I'm sorry that you aren't beautiful.

(*Evenly*)

But yes, I wish you'd go away
And leave me alone!

(*Quietly; intense*)

Everywhere I turn,
There you are.
This is not love,
But some kind of obsession.

Will you never learn
When too far is too far,
Have you no concern
For what *I* feel,
What *I* want?

Love is what you earn,
And return,
When you care for another
So much that the other's

Set free.
Don't you see?
Can't you understand?

Love's not a constant demand,
It's a gift you bestow.
Love isn't sudden surrender,
It's tender and slow.
It must grow.

(*Increasingly angry*)

Yet everywhere I go,
You appear,
Or I know
You are near.
This is not love,
Just a need for possession.

Call it what you will,
This is not love,
This is the reverse,
Like a curse,
Something out of control.
I've begun to fear for my soul...

(*Music stops; a loud clap of thunder is heard. Trembling,
Fosca rises and begins to leave. She stops, shudders momentarily and, with a muffled cry, crumples to the ground.
Giorgio turns and sees her lying there; he crosses the stage
past her and begins to exit. He stops, pauses for a moment,
then reluctantly returns to her, covering her with his coat.
He picks her up and carries her offstage as the lights fade
to black*)

SCENE TEN

Parade ground.
The Soldiers enter, drilling; drums, then bugle.

TORASSO:
> Both of them were soaked to the skin.

RIZZOLLI:
> Where had they been?

AUGENTI:
> On the bluff.

COOK:
> Were they all alone?

TORASSO:
> No one knows.

COOK:
> You don't suppose—?

BARRI:
> Ugh!

RIZZOLLI:

>Gentlemen, enough!

TORASSO:

>Still, it would explain Signora's attitude—

AUGENTI:

>Why she comes to every meal.

BARRI:

>It isn't for the veal.

TORASSO:

>And it would explain the Colonel's gratitude.

COOK:

>I hear he calls him "Giorgio"—

RIZZOLLI:

>But nobody is that brave.

AUGENTI:

>No, that's cheek.

RIZZOLLI:

>Nobody is that brave.

COOK:

>Wouldn't you like to peek?

TORASSO:

>Ugh!

BARRI:

>Gentlemen, I think I'll change my wager:

He'll be Major
Next week.

RIZZOLLI:
I'll say!

ALL (*Except Rizzolli*): I'll say!

ALL:
I'll say!

(*A bed is rolled onstage. At first we can't quite make out who is in it: we see a black-caped form writhing as the bed spins. The black figure lifts up: it is Fosca atop Giorgio, who struggles beneath; the Soldiers and Attendants surround this action*)

GROUP 1:
Everywhere I turn,

GROUP 2:
Everywhere I turn,

GROUP 1:
There you are.

GROUP 2:
There you are.

GROUPS 1 & 2:
This is not love,
But some kind of obsession.

GROUP 1:
Everywhere I go,

GROUP 2:
> Everywhere I go,

GROUPS 1 & 2:
> You appear,
> Or I know
> You are near.

GROUP 2:
> You are near.

GROUPS 1 & 2:
> You are near.
>
> Love,
> Love's not a constant demand.
> It's a gift you bestow.
> Love isn't sudden—
> It's tender and slow...

GROUP 1:
> Tender and slow...
> Tender and slow...

GROUP 2 (*Overlapping*):
> Sudden surrender...
> Sudden surrender...

> (*All exit including Fosca, who disappears into the shadows
> as the Doctor appears; we are now in Giorgio's bedroom*)

GIORGIO (*In his sleep*): Let go. Let go of me. Help me. Please
help me!

(*The Doctor wakes him*)

What?

DOCTOR: It's all right. Calm down.

GIORGIO: She was dragging me down into the grave with her. She was hugging me. Kissing me with her cold lips. Those thin arms pulling me, drawing me, like icy tentacles.

DOCTOR: It was only a dream.

GIORGIO: I feel so warm.

DOCTOR: You became ill after carrying Signora Fosca back in the rain.

GIORGIO: When was that?

DOCTOR: Two days ago.

(*He puts his hand to Giorgio's head*)

You still have a fever, but it seems to be lower. My boy, you will recover from this illness, but it will take some time. You might as well enjoy it away from here. I am putting you on sick leave.

GIORGIO: Sick leave?

DOCTOR: This is a dreary place. It can get to us all.

(*Understanding the implication, Giorgio looks to the Doctor*)

As soon as you are well enough, you will depart for Milan.

GIORGIO (*Fondly*): Milan...

DOCTOR: Don't look so sad, Captain. I trust there is someone there who can oversee your recuperation.

SCENE ELEVEN

A train compartment.
  Formation takes us from Giorgio's bed to a train compartment.

SOLDIER (*While other Soldiers hum in background*):
  To feel a woman's touch,
  To touch a woman's hand,
  Reminded me how much I long to be with you,
  How long I've been without you near.

  And then to hear a woman's voice,
  To hold a woman's arm,
  To feel a woman's touch...

(*Clara strolls through*)

CLARA:
  Giorgio, darling,
  Forty days' leave so soon!
  Imagine that,
  A whole forty days—
  Well, forty matinees.

I'll be there to greet the train
That carried you away from me
Because it brings you home.

(*Giorgio enters slowly. He has a blanket around him and carries a suitcase as he moves towards the train compartment where he sits*)

I'm filling up the room,
Our little room,
With every flower in bloom.
I'll have the fire lit,
The table set,
I'll wear the blue chemise.

And once we're in our room,
Our secret room,
Where I'll be able to care for you,
Kiss you,
Embrace you,
Be there for you...

(*She exits. The train whistle blows and, just as the train starts to move, Fosca enters, carrying a small suitcase*)

GIORGIO (*Furious*): How could you? How dare you follow me?!

FOSCA: I've come to speak to you.

GIORGIO: I am ill. Do you understand that? And you are the reason I am ill.

FOSCA (*Sitting*): I apologize. Nothing could be further from what I wished for you. That is why I wanted to follow you to Milan. To see that you are well.

GIORGIO: That is the reasoning of a capricious child. You can't do this.

FOSCA: I heard what you said, Giorgio. I've come to tell you I'll keep my distance... stay out of your path. But I can be nearby. I can be there quietly waiting.

GIORGIO: And this you think will make me love you?

FOSCA: No. No, I am doing this because *I* love *you*.

GIORGIO: Well, my heart feels nothing for you. How many times must you hear this?

FOSCA: This has nothing to do with your heart. This has to do with your eyes—what you see. If I were beautiful, if there were ample flesh on my bones, if my breasts were large and full, if I were soft and warm to your touch—you would feel otherwise.

GIORGIO (*Firm*): No. Your appearance is no excuse for the way you behave. My feelings towards you are a result of your relentlessness, your constant selfishness and insensitivity.

FOSCA (*After a pause; music underneath*): I'm sorry. No one has ever taught me how to love. I know I feel too much. I often don't know what to do with my feelings. You understand that, Giorgio. Don't you?

GIORGIO (*Slowly, pleading*): Fosca, you have to face the truth. Please. You have to give me up.

FOSCA (*Calm*):
Loving you
Is not a choice,
It's who I am.

Loving you
Is not a choice
And not much reason
To rejoice,

But it gives me purpose,
Gives me voice,
To say to the world:

This is why I live.
You are why I live.

Loving you
Is why I do
The things I do.

Loving you
Is not in my
Control.

But loving you,
I have a goal
For what's left of my life...

I will live,
And I would die
For you.

(*As music continues under*)

GIORGIO (*Skeptical*): Die for me? What kind of love is that?
FOSCA: The truest love. Would Clara give her life for yours?
Would she, Giorgio?

(*A beat; he doesn't answer, realizing the truth of his situation*)

I would. Happily. In the end, you'll finally see what is beautiful about me. (*Beat*) Do you want me to move to another compartment?
GIORGIO: We're getting off at the next stop. I'm taking you back.

(*She turns from him and stares out the window; after a beat, she begins to shiver from the cold*)

You're freezing.

(*No response*)

Cover yourself up.

(*She doesn't move*)

Do you want to get sicker?

(*She still doesn't respond; he moves to her and wraps his blanket around her*)

FOSCA (*Staring out the window*): The moonlight makes even this landscape look lovely.

(*He returns to his seat*)

Look. There seem to be faces in those rocks, smiling back at us.

(*Slowly, Giorgio looks out to see what she sees; he smiles ever so slightly, then slowly turns back to look at Fosca as the lights fade to black*)

WOMAN (*Offstage*):
    How long were we apart...

MAN (*Offstage*):
    A month, a week, a day?

WOMAN (*Offstage*):
    To feel your touch again...

BOTH (*Offstage*):
    You've never been away...

(*Lights up on the courtyard where Giorgio is met by the Doctor; Giorgio remains weak, his illness very apparent*)

DOCTOR: Don't be offended if I'm amused, Captain, but it is all quite bizarre, really. She led you back like a lamb.

GIORGIO: You know her, and you know there is no way I could have acted differently.

DOCTOR: You needn't worry. No one knows of her exploits.

GIORGIO: I suppose I should be relieved, though in truth it matters little to me.

(*Turning on him*)

And who told her I was leaving?

DOCTOR (*Defensive*): I hardly thought it a secret.

GIORGIO: What is it that you want, Doctor?

DOCTOR: I don't know what you mean.

GIORGIO: You know what I mean. Why did you bring this woman into my life?

DOCTOR: I thought it would help her. I thought it might bring her some small degree of happiness....I had no intention for it to turn to this, Captain. Honestly, I didn't. I apologize.

(*Giorgio begins to leave*)

She tells me that you're going to Milan tomorrow, but for only four days. I assume that is just a pretext and that you won't be coming back?

GIORGIO: I don't want to be away from my duties that long. Excuse me, I have things to do. (*Walks away*)

DOCTOR: Captain Bachetti, you forget that I am *your* superior. You can't decide to forgo a sick leave just like that. Has Signora Fosca brought you to this point?

GIORGIO: Absolutely not. This is my decision.

DOCTOR: Don't you see what she is doing to you? To your mental state? I may have helped bring this woman into your life, but I can also get you away from her. For your own good. I can see to it that you are transferred permanently. If I send a dispatch to headquarters, you'll be *ordered* to leave.

GIORGIO: I don't wish to be transferred.

DOCTOR: Why are you behaving this way?

GIORGIO (*After a moment*): I feel it my duty to help her.

DOCTOR: Don't you understand, Captain? No one can help her. Good day.

(*The Doctor exits. The Soldiers enter drunkenly; they quiet when they see Giorgio, who acknowledges them and then exits*)

TORASSO:

Forty days—!

COOK:

Where does he get all the luck?

TORASSO:

Forty days—!

RIZZOLLI:

The man is sick.

TORASSO:

But forty days—!

BARRI:

> Yes, he's sick of being stuck
> In the sticks.

AUGENTI:

> Who isn't?

TORASSO:

> In Milan—!

COOK:

> He's gone
> Because it's getting pretty thick
> With the Signora.

RIZZOLLI:

> Gentlemen—

AUGENTI:

> He'd better get out quick
> From the Signora.

RIZZOLLI:

> Gentlemen—

BARRI:

> That's not an easy trick
> With the Signora.

RIZZOLLI (*Loudly*):

> Gentlemen!

> (*They turn to him*)

You know what I think?
We need another drink!

COOK: I'll say.

RIZZOLLI:
I'll say!

ALL:
I'll say!
I'll say!
I'll—

(*They look at each other and walk off in disgust*)

SCENE TWELVE

Near the Milan train station.
   Clara and Giorgio stroll from the train station to a
bench nearby; music under.

CLARA:
   Giorgio,
   I didn't tell you in my letter
   Something even better,
   A surprise here at home:
   In a week my husband goes to Rome.
   It's the first time he's away,
   He'll be gone at least a day,
   Maybe two or even three.

   I can visit you at night,
   We'll be lighted by the moon,
   Not a shuttered afternoon.

   Just think of having time
   That we can call our own,
   Together and alone.

> Perhaps we'll take a drive
> Into the country,
> And perhaps at last
> We'll share a sunrise.
> Wouldn't that be beautiful—?

GIORGIO: Clara, I'm not taking my sick leave.

CLARA: What do you mean?

GIORGIO: I'm staying only four days.

CLARA (*Jealous*): It's that woman, isn't it?

GIORGIO: There are many reasons—

CLARA: No! You constantly write to me about her, speak of her when we're together. She's always on your mind, Giorgio. Do you love her?

GIORGIO: The idea is laughable.

CLARA: I hate this woman, and I don't even know her.

GIORGIO: There are times when I hate her, too.

CLARA: Then why do you sacrifice yourself on her behalf?

(*A beat*)

GIORGIO: I'm not certain. Clara, please don't be angry. This woman has no friends. No one to talk to. I know the power I have over her. I didn't ask for this power—she bestowed it upon me, but somehow it carries responsibilities that I can't seem to shed.

CLARA: She needs you.

GIORGIO: Don't you need me, too?

CLARA: Yes, of course, but not like this woman.

GIORGIO: Leave your husband, Clara.

CLARA (*Stunned*): What?

GIORGIO: Let's have a life together.

CLARA (*Slowly*): Giorgio, you know that's not possible.

GIORGIO: Everything is possible.

CLARA: I would lose my child.

GIORGIO: And what if you were to lose me?

CLARA: I don't want to lose you, Giorgio. You knew my situation.

GIORGIO: We could run away together. We could take your child—

CLARA: You're not thinking clearly. You're not yourself.

GIORGIO (*Defensive*): I'm myself!

CLARA: Where would we go? How would we live?

GIORGIO: We would manage.

CLARA: We are not two people who could ever just "manage." We have to carve out a life for ourselves around our present obligations. We have no choice.

GIORGIO: We have a choice.

CLARA: Yes, I suppose that's true, Giorgio. Just as you have chosen to forgo your sick leave.

(*He is surprised by her remark; they look at one another awkwardly*)

I've often wondered if you would love me as much if I were free.

GIORGIO: I would. You know I would. I love you.

CLARA: And I love you. (*Beat*) You're not coming back, are you?

GIORGIO: I'll be back, Clara. I'll be back. Let's stop this talk and enjoy our four days together.

SCENE THIRTEEN

The Colonel's dining room.
We segue to a Christmas party in the dining quarters with all the Soldiers, household staff, the Colonel and the Doctor. Fosca plays the piano as Torasso sings a Christmas carol.

TORASSO (*Singing*):
> La pace sulla terra
> È a voi tranquilità.
> È nato un bambino
> Che il mondo salverà
> Dal gran poter di Sàtan
> E da sua potestà.
> O novella di gran felicità!

(*His grand ending is met with enthusiasm*)

COLONEL: Thank you, Lieutenant. (*To Fosca*) That was beautiful, my dear. (*To all*) Merry Christmas, everyone. *Salute.*
ALL: *Salute!*
RIZZOLLI: When is dinner being served, Sergeant Lombardi?
COOK: The pheasants will be ready shortly.

COLONEL: The Christmas season is the most wonderful time of the year, wouldn't you agree, Doctor?

DOCTOR: I am not much of a believer, I must confess.

COLONEL: It isn't the birth of Christ we're celebrating tonight. We are celebrating the joys of domestic life.

COOK: And the food!

COLONEL: All right, yes, the food.

(Colonel declines more Champagne from the Cook)

No, thank you.

(Giorgio enters, still looking somewhat ill)

Look who has arrived.

(The Colonel, with Fosca on his arm, crosses to Giorgio)

DOCTOR: Captain.

COLONEL: Thank you for coming, Captain. I am so happy that you haven't taken your leave.

(Augenti enters with a stack of letters, which he distributes)

AUGENTI: Mail.

COLONEL: We've come to think of you as part of the family.

RIZZOLLI: At last, a letter for me.

GIORGIO: And I appreciate that.

AUGENTI: Colonel.

COLONEL: Excuse me. *(He takes his mail and backs off)*

FOSCA: Are you feeling better, Captain?

GIORGIO: Yes, thank you.

FOSCA: It's kind of you to join us tonight.

GIORGIO: My pleasure. You look very charming.

FOSCA (*Uncomfortable*): Thank you.

AUGENTI: Captain.

(*He gives Giorgio a letter; there is an awkward moment between Fosca and Giorgio*)

FOSCA: Go ahead, Captain. Read your letter. It's fine. (*She retreats to the Doctor's side*)

BARRI: I can smell the perfume on Captain Bachetti's letter from here. And fragrant perfume it is, Captain. My correspondence smells like it came from the barn.

(*Barri engages Giorgio in conversation*)

COOK: Dinner will be ready in ten minutes. I've just put in the truffles.

RIZZOLLI: Truffles, indeed. I can't remember the last time I had truffles.

TORASSO: I hope they'll be recognizable after Sergeant Lombardi...

COLONEL: Captain Bachetti—

(*Giorgio realizes the Colonel is addressing him*)

Is it you or the gentlemen from the ministry who are responsible for this surprise?

(*A hush falls over the room*)

GIORGIO: Excuse me?

COLONEL: You have been transferred back to headquarters. You are to report immediately.

GIORGIO (*Taken completely by surprise*): Immediately?

COLONEL: This is most unusual, Captain Bachetti.

GIORGIO: Really, I don't understand.

(*His eyes go from the Doctor to Fosca, who stands stunned for a moment*)

FOSCA (*Emotional*): Giorgio! (*As she crosses to him*) My love, don't leave!

(*She throws herself into his arms; there is an embarrassing moment as everyone in the room tries to hide his discomfort*)

COLONEL (*As if to an errant child*): Fosca!

(*She turns and looks to the others, who all stare at her. She runs offstage with a scream, pushing away anyone in her path; the Doctor follows*)

Gentlemen.

(*The others in the room exit as the Colonel moves to Giorgio*)

You will wait here for me, Captain Bachetti.

(*The Colonel exits after Fosca; Giorgio pauses in confusion, then crosses to a chair and sits, staring off into space. Clara enters; music under*)

CLARA:
 Giorgio...

(*He stares*)

 Giorgio...

(Suddenly he remembers Clara's letter; he opens it and begins to read)

I am writing to you,
My angel,
Though not long since you've been gone,
With a most unhappy heart.

Because, in truth, as time goes on,
I think of nothing else but you—
And us.

Oh, my love, my sweet,
You've changed,
I've watched you change.
You're not the man I thought I knew.

At times, these past few days together,
I would wonder whether
You were here,
Really here with me.

I thought, was I naive
To believe
We'd continue year by year?
Is it over forever?

(Music stops)

It seems to me the answer rests with you. Yes, I have obligations at home, but my heart is yours. When my son is older, when he goes off to school, there is the chance for us to be together. I will make the sacrifice you ask of me then. Please understand why I can't now. Will you wait for me,

Giorgio? Can we have back what we once had? I have to know. We both have to know.

(*Music resumes*)

GIORGIO (*Bitterly, quietly*):
Just another love story.

CLARA:
No one is to blame.

GIORGIO:
A temporary love story.

CLARA:
But it needn't end the same.

GIORGIO:
I thought we had more.

CLARA:
We had more—

GIORGIO:
We had something more—

BOTH:
—Than any other love story.

CLARA:
All that happiness—

GIORGIO (*Looking at the letter*):
Is this what you call love?

CLARA:
> —We had then—

GIORGIO:
> This logical and sensible
> Practical arrangement—

CLARA (*Overlapping*):
> We can have that happiness—

GIORGIO:
> —This foregone conclusion—

CLARA:
> —Once again!

GIORGIO:
> —You think that this is love?

(*His voice rising, he crumples the letter*)

> Love isn't so convenient.
> Love isn't something scheduled in advance,
> Not something guaranteed
> You need
> For fear it may pass you by.
> You have to take a chance,
> You can't just try it out.
> What's love unless it's unconditional?
>
> Love doesn't give a damn about tomorrow,
> And neither do I!

CLARA:
> All that happiness—

GIORGIO:

It was fine.

CLARA:

—In the past—

GIORGIO:

I was yours, you were mine.

CLARA:

That was not just happiness,
Love was in that happiness,
That's why it will last.

GIORGIO:

Love is more, I want more.

BOTH:

I thought I knew what love was—

CLARA:

I didn't know that love was a complication.

GIORGIO:

I do know that it's not a negotiation.

CLARA:

We'll take it in our stride.

GIORGIO:

What we had—

CLARA:

You decide.

GIORGIO:
> —Wasn't bad.

CLARA:
> We could have everything.
> I want you more than anything.

GIORGIO:
> How sad—

CLARA:
> To wait is nothing.
> We're young, and time is nothing.

GIORGIO:
> —That what we have is nothing...

CLARA:
> Nothing...

BOTH:
> Nothing...

(She disappears as the Colonel enters, brandishing a piece of paper)

COLONEL: Signor Bachetti—

(Giorgio stands)

I discovered this letter at my cousin's bedside. This *is* your signature, is it not?

GIORGIO (*Uncomfortable*): Yes, sir.

COLONEL (*Cold*): You have taken advantage of my cousin's affections.

GIORGIO: That was not my intention, sir. Perhaps you should discuss this matter with Signora Fosca.

COLONEL: My cousin is asleep, and in any event, I wouldn't subject her to such a question. No one can make me believe that a man such as yourself would desire a woman like Signora Fosca, would write her a letter like this.

GIORGIO (*After a pause*): Why is that, sir?

COLONEL: The reason seems obvious.

GIORGIO: Not to me. Forgive me for saying this, but you had no right to read that letter—no right to take it from her room.

(*He goes to grab the letter, but the Colonel angrily pulls it back*)

COLONEL: My cousin is at the end of her life. She does not deserve to be led on in such a manner!

GIORGIO: You don't know your cousin. She is not a child! She is not just a sick person. Signora Fosca is as responsible for her actions as am I for mine.

COLONEL: You have abused my good faith, come into my house to dishonor it. Your attitude towards me is nothing short of contemptuous. I must demand a reparation from you—and mere words will not suffice.

GIORGIO: What? Fight? A duel?

COLONEL: I have confided in you. You know that my cousin has been taken advantage of before.

(*The Doctor enters and stands off to the side*)

We will meet tomorrow morning at eight, behind the castle steps.

DOCTOR (*Trying to make light of the situation*): Gentlemen, wait. Colonel, there is an explanation. Captain Bachetti, speak up. Say how she forced you—

GIORGIO: Not at all. Nothing was forced on me.

DOCTOR: Please, let's come to our senses here.

COLONEL: And one more thing.

GIORGIO: Yes?

COLONEL: My cousin knows nothing of this discovery. She must know nothing of what is going to happen. I need your word on that.

GIORGIO: She will not hear of this matter from me.

COLONEL: Very well. Tomorrow. (*He exits*)

DOCTOR: It's deplorable that that woman has brought you to this. Let's not panic. The Colonel will calm down. There's still time to explain—

GIORGIO: I wish to see Fosca.

DOCTOR: What?

GIORGIO: Whatever the outcome of this duel, I'll never see her again. Arrange for me to meet her tonight as you did before.

DOCTOR: You don't know what you're saying.

GIORGIO: You may have forgotten how to cure diseases, but you induced mine, so don't pretend you don't know what I'm saying.

DOCTOR: You understand this woman could never be your lover. Her physical condition—

GIORGIO: You *will* arrange for me to see her, Doctor.

DOCTOR: No! I will not participate in this madness.

(*The Doctor exits; music; we segue to Fosca's bedroom*)

SCENE FOURTEEN

Fosca's bedroom.

   Quietly, Giorgio enters. Fosca is resting on the bed and doesn't hear him.

GIORGIO: Fosca. Fosca.

(*She lifts herself up*)

I'm sorry to surprise you like this.

FOSCA: Thank you for coming.

GIORGIO: I wanted you to know that I had nothing to do with the transfer.

FOSCA (*She rises*): I know that now. The Doctor told me.

GIORGIO (*Beat*): The letter from Clara...

FOSCA: Yes?

GIORGIO: It's over. Finished.

FOSCA (*Another beat*): I'm sorry.

GIORGIO (*Surprised*): Sorry? I would have thought you would be pleased.

FOSCA: There was a time when I would have welcomed that news, but I realize I don't wish you to be unhappy. I don't wish to see you sad.

GIORGIO: I feel so much...but I'm not really sad.

FOSCA: I thought you loved Clara?

GIORGIO: I did love Clara. I did. But... (*Quietly at first*)
No one has ever loved me
As deeply as you.
No one has truly loved me
As you have, Fosca.

(*Stronger*)

Love without reason, love without mercy,
Love without pride or shame.
Love unconcerned
With being returned—
No wisdom, no judgment,
No caution, no blame.

No one has ever known me
As clearly as you.
No one has ever shown me
What love could be like until now:

Not pretty or safe or easy,
But more than I ever knew.
Love within reason—that isn't love.

And I've learned that from you...

(*Music continues under; he sees her trembling*)

Are you cold?

FOSCA: No, I'm afraid.

GIORGIO: Of what?

FOSCA:

> All this happiness,
> Coming when there's so little time.
> Too much happiness,
> More than I can bear.

(*Music continues under*)

> I pray for the strength to enjoy it. Tomorrow you will leave.
> This is the only time I have. (*Beat*) You do love me, don't
> you?

GIORGIO (*Slowly, amazed at the realization*): Yes, I love you.

FOSCA: Say it again.

GIORGIO (*Firm*): I love you.

FOSCA: Once more.

GIORGIO (*Embracing her as she breaks down*): I love you. Be
  calm. Strong. I am yours.

FOSCA: This isn't a dream?

GIORGIO: This isn't a dream.

(*She begins to lead him towards the bed but Giorgio resists*)

> We can't.

FOSCA: To die loved is to have lived.

(*They kiss. Fosca becomes weak, and Giorgio lifts her and
carries her to the bed where he gently puts her down. He
stares at her momentarily; her strength returns and she
pulls him onto the bed as the music swells and the lights
fade*)

SCENE FIFTEEN

An open field.
    *We hear the sound of military drums. Daybreak. The
Colonel, the Doctor, Torasso, Barri, the Cook, Augenti and
two Soldiers march in and take their positions. Giorgio and
Rizzolli enter last; Giorgio looks hollow-eyed and dishev-
elled.*

COOK: Gentlemen.

(*The Colonel crosses to center; Giorgio stands numb*)

DOCTOR: Captain.

(*Giorgio comes to life and makes his way to center; the
Cook presents a box with the pistols. Giorgio and the
Colonel each take one and then move to their positions*)

TORASSO: Gentlemen. Ten paces, please. One, two, three, four,
five, six, seven, eight, nine, ten.

(*The Colonel and Giorgio mark off ten paces. They turn
and fire simultaneously. The Colonel stands frozen for an*

instant, then trembles and falls to the ground; the Doctor and the other men rush to his aid, leaving Giorgio standing alone on the other side of the stage. Suddenly, Giorgio lets out a high-pitched howl — a cry that is clearly reminiscent of Fosca's — as lights fade to black)

SCENE SIXTEEN

A hospital.

   Lights up on Giorgio, dazed, sitting at a desk. A nurse enters and brings him a box with a letter. As Giorgio opens the letter, the Doctor enters.

DOCTOR: Captain Bachetti. I didn't write to you before, because I knew your illness might prevent you from comprehending the contents of my letter. I now have heard that you are closer to recovery and that your nervous condition has improved.

    I don't know exactly what you have been told, or what you even remember of the events that led you away. Signora Fosca died three days after the night you last saw one another. She died unaware of what took place between you and her cousin. The Colonel's wound was serious, but not mortal. He recovered in a few months. I wanted to speak to the Colonel about you in order to convince him of your innocence, but in the end I worried that I would hurt your cause more than help it.

    In a box that I am mailing, you will find papers that were left behind in your desk. Also, I have enclosed some personal belongings of Signora Fosca's, and a letter she wrote you just prior to her death.

(*As Giorgio goes through the papers in the box, he summons up his past*)

BARRI, RIZZOLLI & TORASSO:
    The town, it is remote, isn't it?
    And provincial—
    Don't you think?

CLARA (*Overlapping*):
    I'm filling up our room,
    Our little room,
    With every flower in bloom.
    I'll have the fire lit,
    The table set,
    I'll wear the blue chemise...

LUDOVIC (*Overlapping*):
    The time has come to face the truth,
    Signorina.

ATTENDANTS (*Overlapping*):
    This sterile little town,
    These pompous little men,

COOK, AUGENTI & SOLDIER I (*Overlapping*):
    This military madness...

ATTENDANTS (*Overlapping*):
    Military madness...

COOK, AUGENTI, SOLDIER I & ATTENDANTS (*Overlapping*):
    Uniforms, uniforms...

CLARA (*Overlapping*):
　　Imagining your fingers touching mine.
　　Imagining our room,
　　The bed,
　　The secrecy,
　　The world outside,
　　Your mouth on mine...

COLONEL (*Overlapping*):
　　An unattractive woman
　　Is easily deceived...

(*Giorgio picks up Fosca's letter, opens it and starts to read*)

GIORGIO: My dearest Giorgio. The end is near. The time has
　　come for me to surrender life gracefully. These past two days
　　since you have left, since we were together, have been a rev-
　　elation.

　　Now at last
　　I see what comes
　　From feeling loved.

　　Strange, how merely
　　Feeling loved,
　　You see things clearly.

(*Fosca's voice quietly begins to join his from offstage*)

　　Things I feared,
　　Like the world itself,
　　I now love dearly.

(*Fosca enters and crosses to him*)

BOTH:

> I want to live.
> Now I want to live,

FOSCA:

> Just from being loved.
>
> All that pain
> I nursed inside
> For all those years—

GIORGIO:

> All that vain
> And bitter self-concern—

BOTH:

> All those tears
> And all that pride
> Have vanished into air...

FOSCA:

> I don't want to leave.

GIORGIO:

> Now that I am loved,

FOSCA:

> I don't want to leave.

BOTH:

> Everywhere I turn,
> You are there.

FOSCA:

> Everywhere I look,
> Things are different.

BOTH:

> Everything seems right,
> Everything seems possible,
> Every moment bursts with feeling.
>
> Why is love so easy to give
> And so hard to receive?

FOSCA:

> But though I want to live,
> I now can leave
> With what I never knew:
> I'm someone to be loved.

GIORGIO:

> I'm someone to be loved.

FOSCA:

> And that I learned from you.

(*The Company becomes visible behind them*)

ALL:

> I don't know how I let you
> So far inside my mind,
> But there you are, and there you will stay.
> How could I ever wish you away?
> I see now I was blind.

FOSCA:

> And should you die tomorrow,
> Another thing I see:

GIORGIO:
>   Your love will live in me....

FOSCA:
>   Your love will live in me....

GIORGIO & GROUP I:
>   Your love will live in me...

FOSCA & GROUP 2:
>   Your love will live in me...

GIORGIO & GROUP I:
>   Your love will live in me...

FOSCA & GROUP 2:
>   Your love will live in me...

GIORGIO & GROUP I:
>   Your love will live in me...

FOSCA & GROUP 2:
>   Your love will live in me...

GIORGIO:
>   Your love will live in me...

FOSCA:
>   Your love will live in me...

GIORGIO:
>   Your love will live in me...

(The Company, Fosca last, leaves Giorgio alone at his desk as the lights fade to black)